TRACE AND LEARN
NUMBERS!

PETER PAUPER PRESS, INC.
White Plains, New York

PETER PAUPER PRESS

In 1928, at the age of twenty-two, Peter Beilenson began printing books on a small press in the basement of his parents' home in Larchmont, New York. Peter—and later, his wife, Edna—sought to create fine books that sold at "prices even a pauper could afford."

Today, still family owned and operated, Peter Pauper Press continues to honor our founders' legacy of quality, value, and fun for big kids and small kids alike.

Images used under license from Shutterstock.com

Designed by Margaret Rubiano

Copyright © 2019
Peter Pauper Press, Inc.
Manufactured for Peter Pauper Press, Inc.
202 Mamaroneck Avenue
White Plains, NY 10601 USA
All rights reserved
ISBN 978-1-4413-3112-0
Printed in China

Published in the United Kingdom and Europe by
Peter Pauper Press, Inc. c/o White Pebble International
Unit 2, Plot 11 Terminus Road
Chichester, West Sussex PO19 8TX, UK

7 6 5 4 3 2 1

Visit us at www.peterpauper.com

·············· INTRODUCTION ··············

This book helps children teach themselves their numbers or practice the number-writing skills they already have. With helpful diagrams, plenty of space to trace and practice, and fun and simple exercises, this is the perfect companion for preschoolers.

Here's what's inside:

Meet the Numbers!

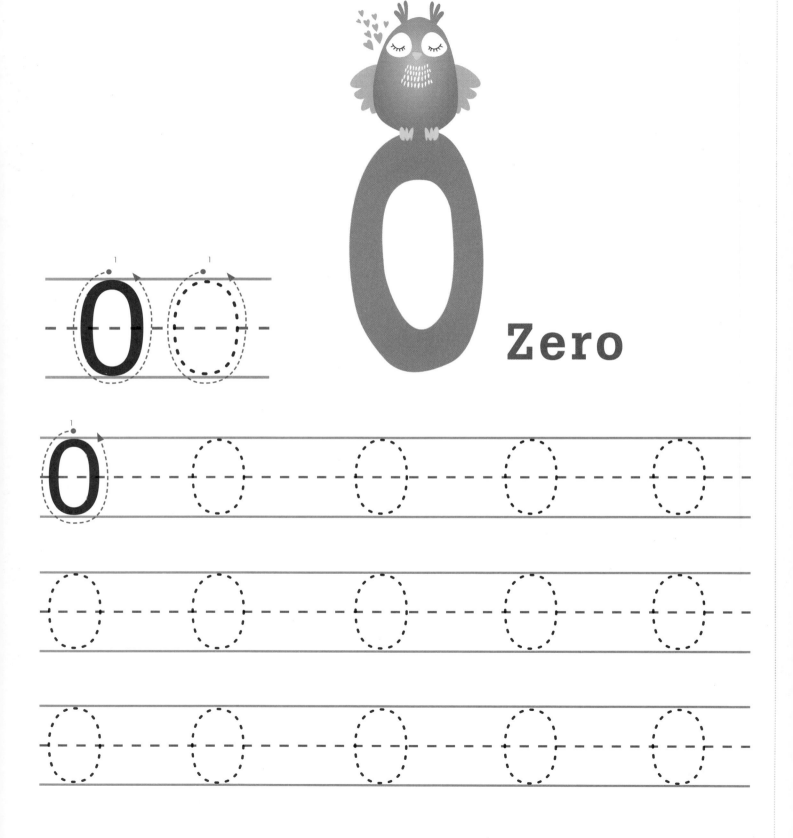

0 Zero

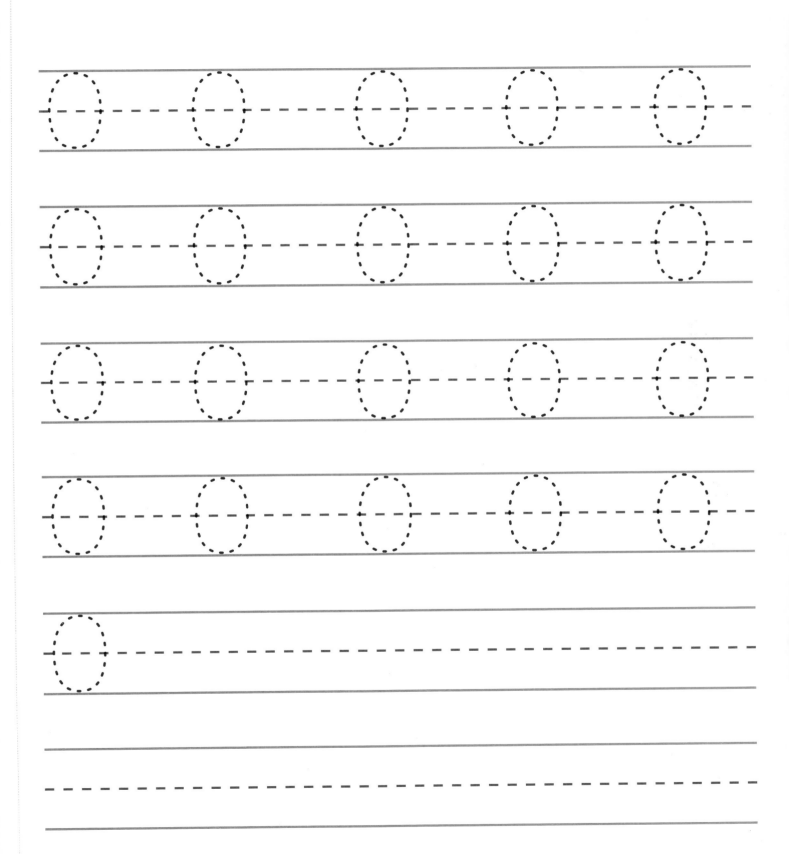

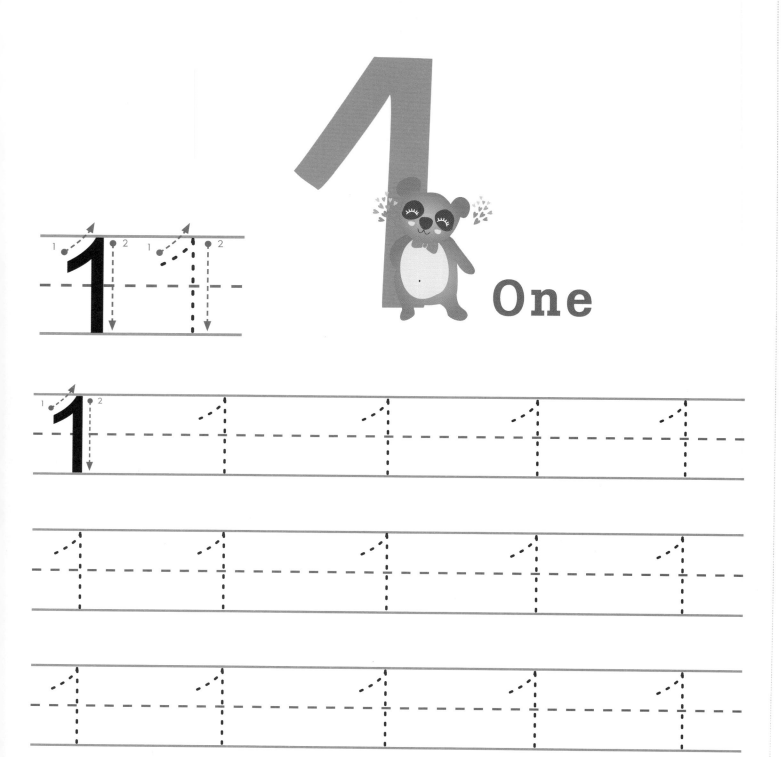

One

2 2

Two

2

2 2 2 2 2

2 2 2 2 2

2 2 2 2 2

2 2 2 2 2

2 2 2 2 2

2 2 2 2 2

2 2 2 2 2

2

Three

3 3 3 3 3 3 3

3 3 3 3 3

3 3 3 3 3

3 3 3 3 3

3 3 3 3 3

3 3 3 3 3

3 3 3 3 3

3

Four

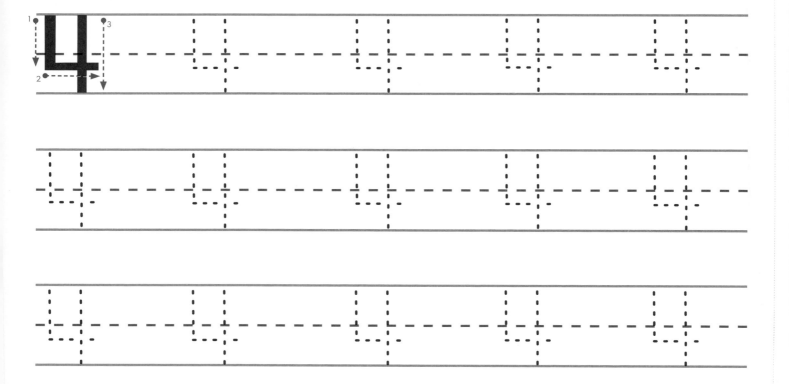

4 4 4 4 4

4 4 4 4 4

4 4 4 4 4

4 4 4 4 4

4

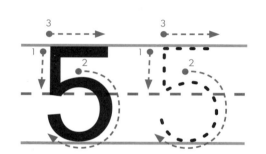

 **Five**

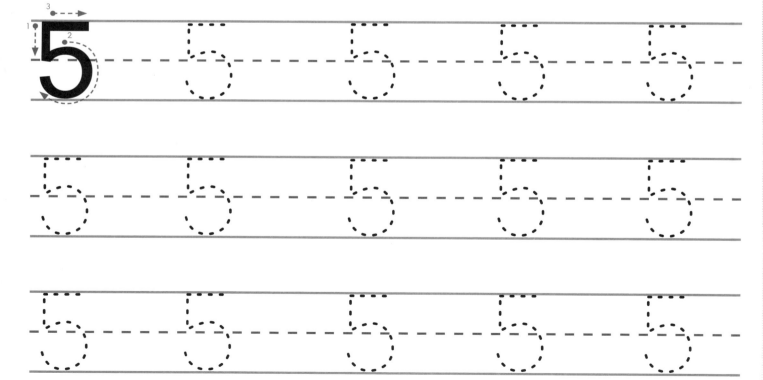

5 5 5 5 5

5 5 5 5 5

5 5 5 5 5

5 5 5 5 5

5

6 6

Six

6

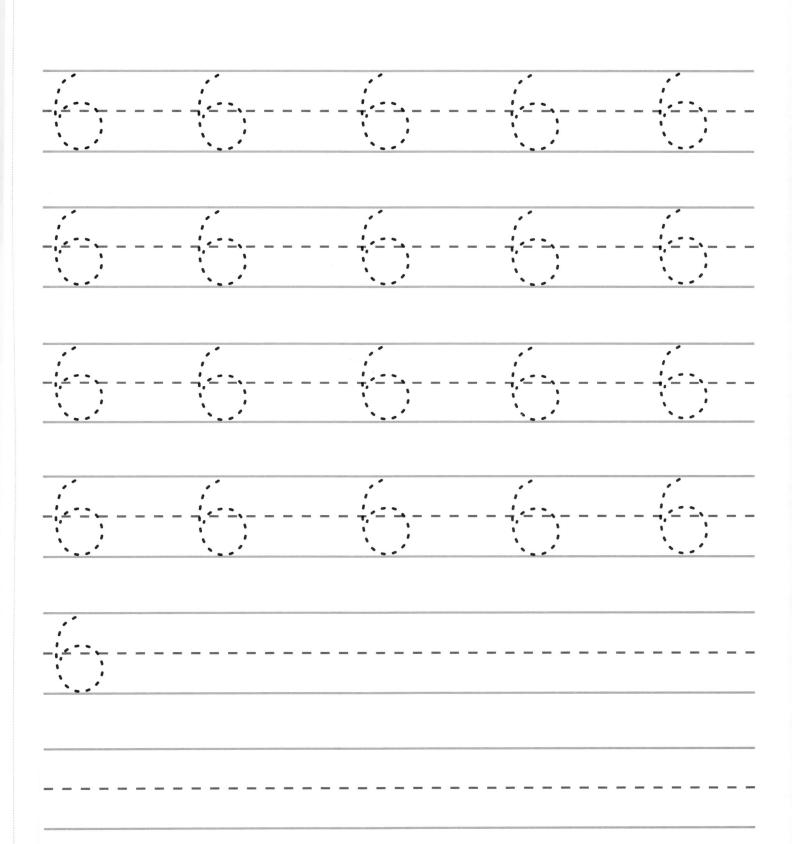

Seven

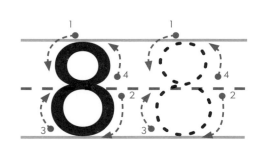

Eight

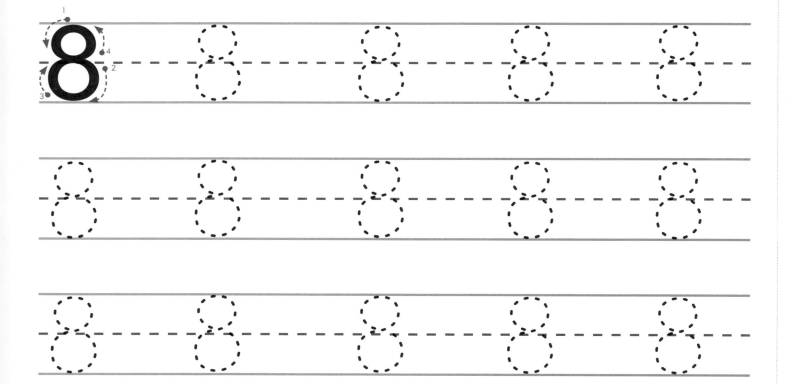

Nine

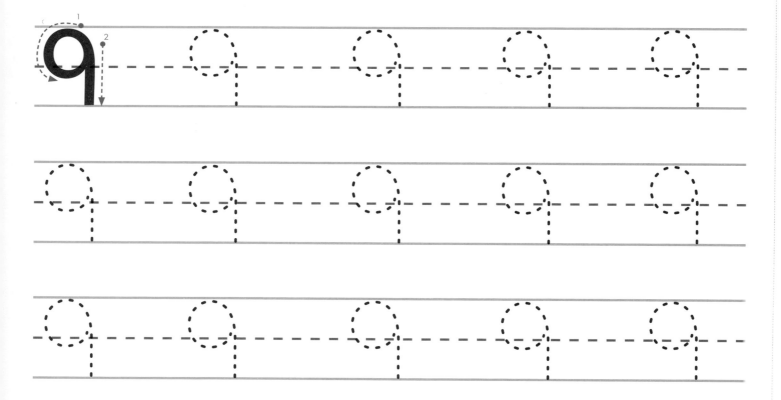

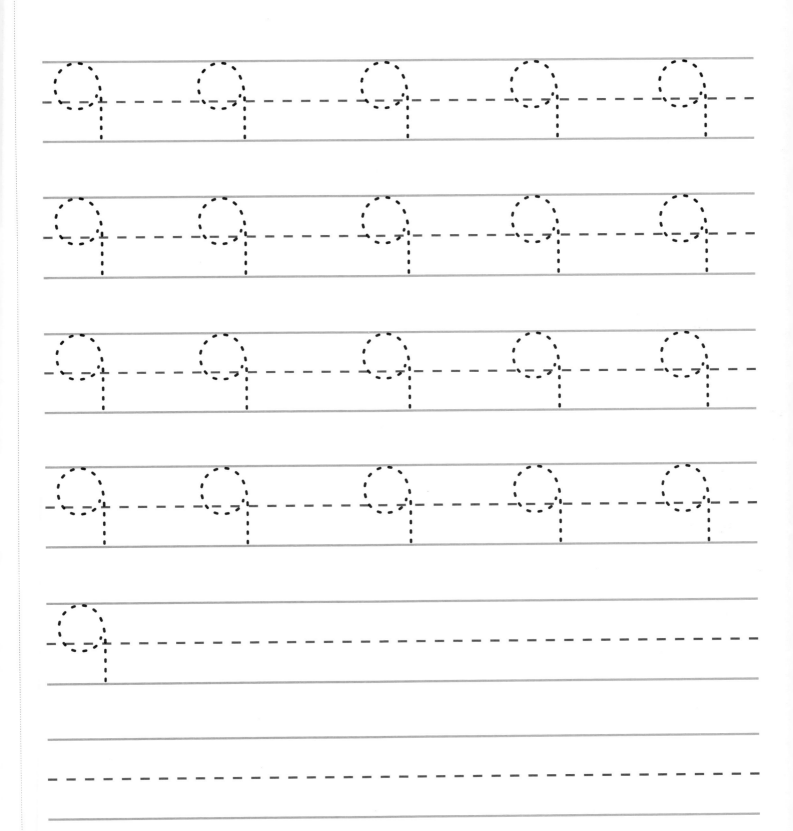

Ten

10 10 10 10 10

10 10 10 10 10

10 10 10 10 10

10 10 10 10 10

10

How Many Do You See?

 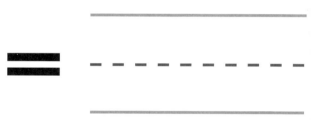

 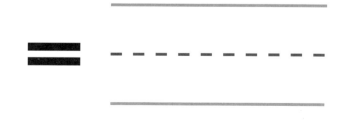

How Many of Each?

How Many  = _ _ _ _ _ _ _ _ _ _ _

How Many 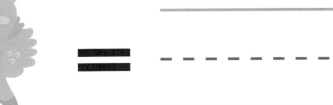 = _ _ _ _ _ _ _ _ _ _ _

How Many  = _ _ _ _ _ _ _ _ _ _ _

How Many Do You See?

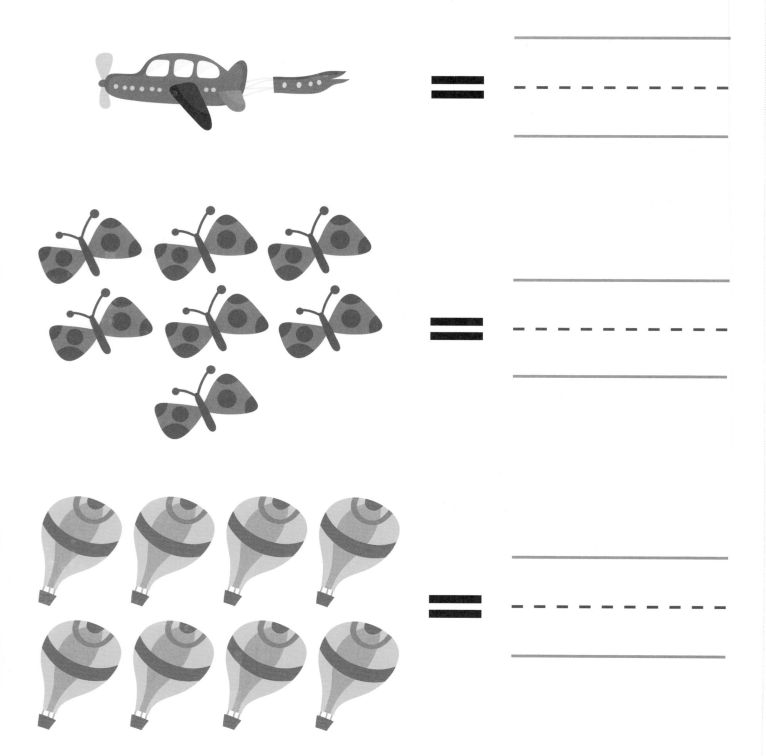

How Many of Each?

How Many  = - - - - - - - - - -

How Many  = - - - - - - - - - -

How Many  = - - - - - - - - - -

Can You Add These Together?

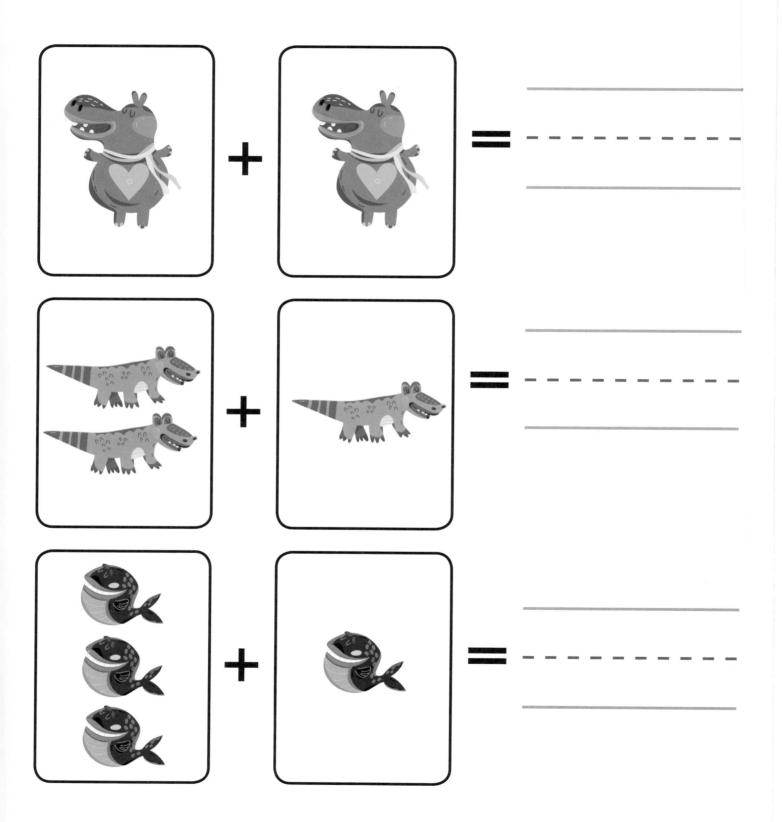

Can You Add These Together?

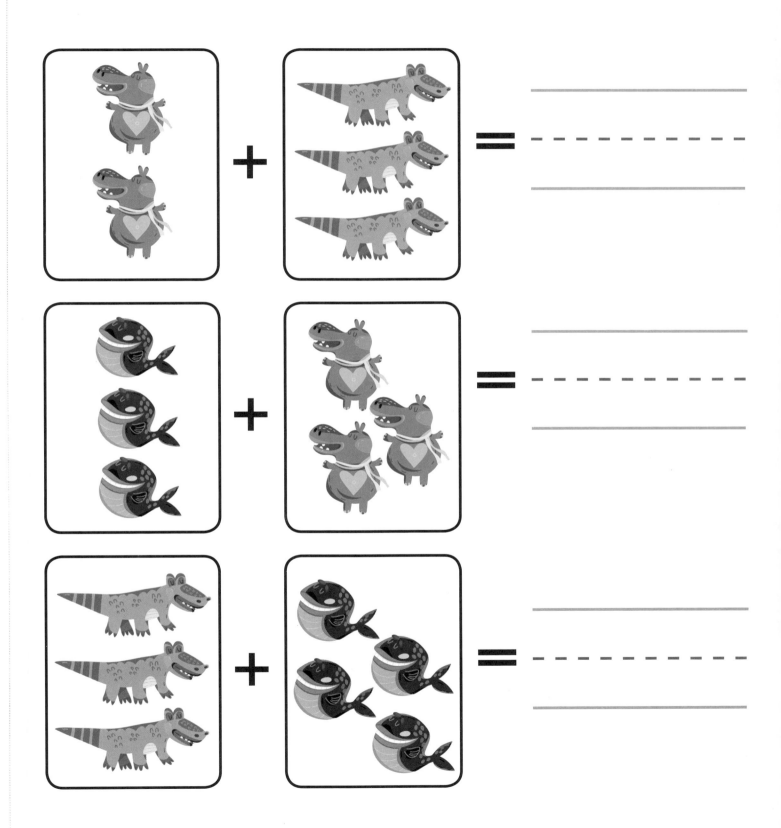

Count the Flowers.
Draw a Line to the Correct Number.

5

3

1

2

4

Count the Strawberries.
Draw a Line to the Correct Number.

4

2

5

1

3

Count the Pictures.
Circle the Correct Number.

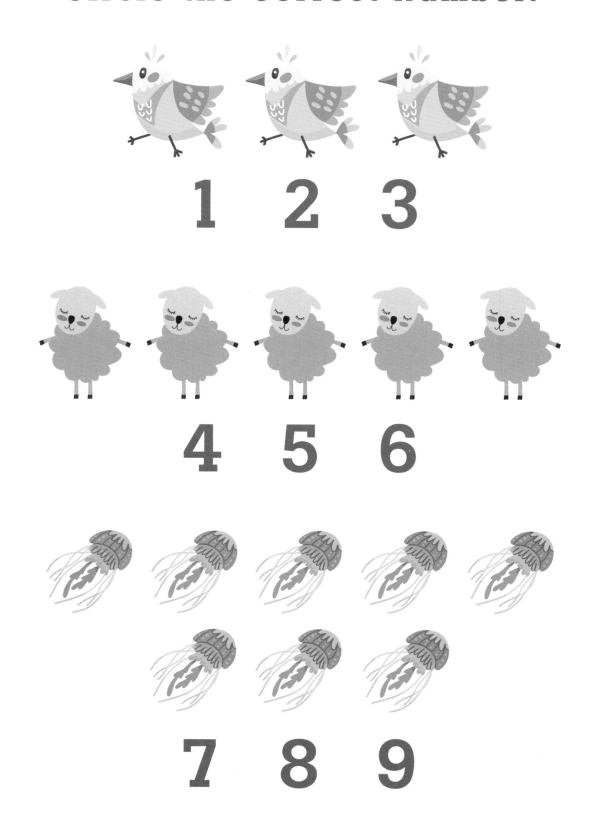

1 2 3

4 5 6

7 8 9

Count the Pictures.
Circle the Correct Number.

1 2 3

4 5 6

7 8 9

How Many Do You See?

How Many Do You See?

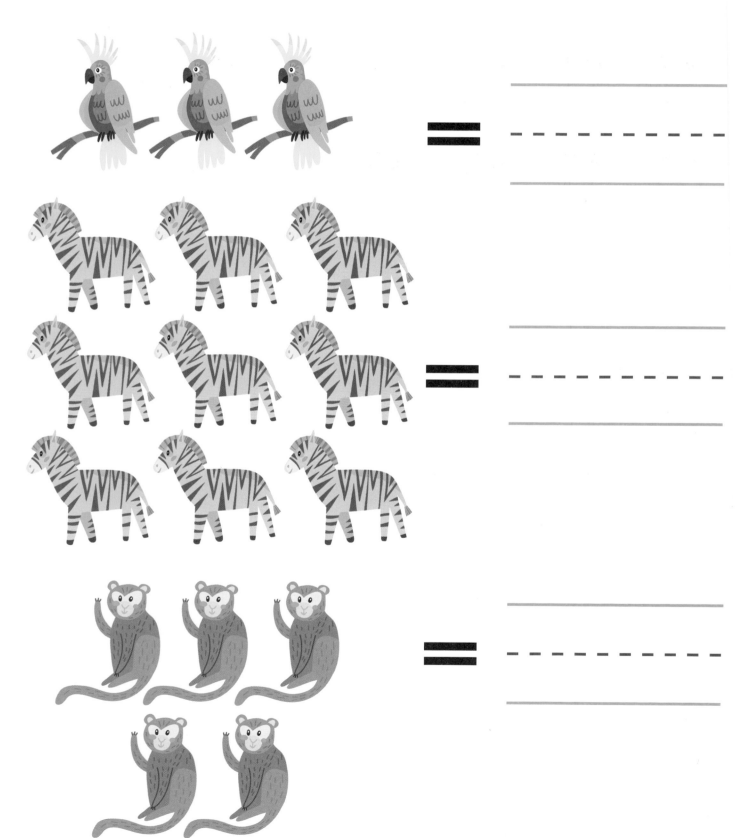

How Many of Each?

How Many 🦜 **=** ---------------

How Many 🦓 **=** ---------------

How Many 🐒 **=** ---------------

Follow the Dots.

Follow the Dots.

Count to 20.

One

1

2

Two

2 2 2 2 2

2 2 2 2 2

3

Three

3

Four

5

Five

6

Six

7

Seven

7

Eight

9

Nine

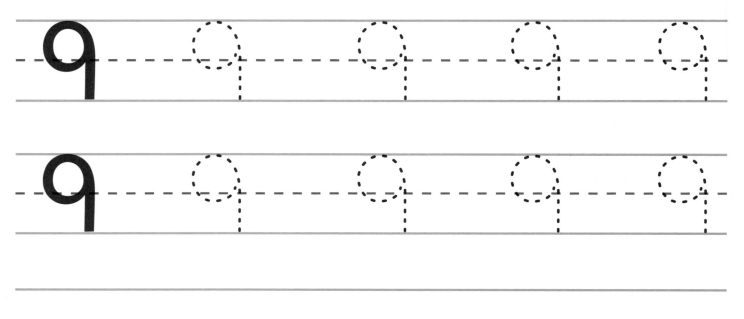

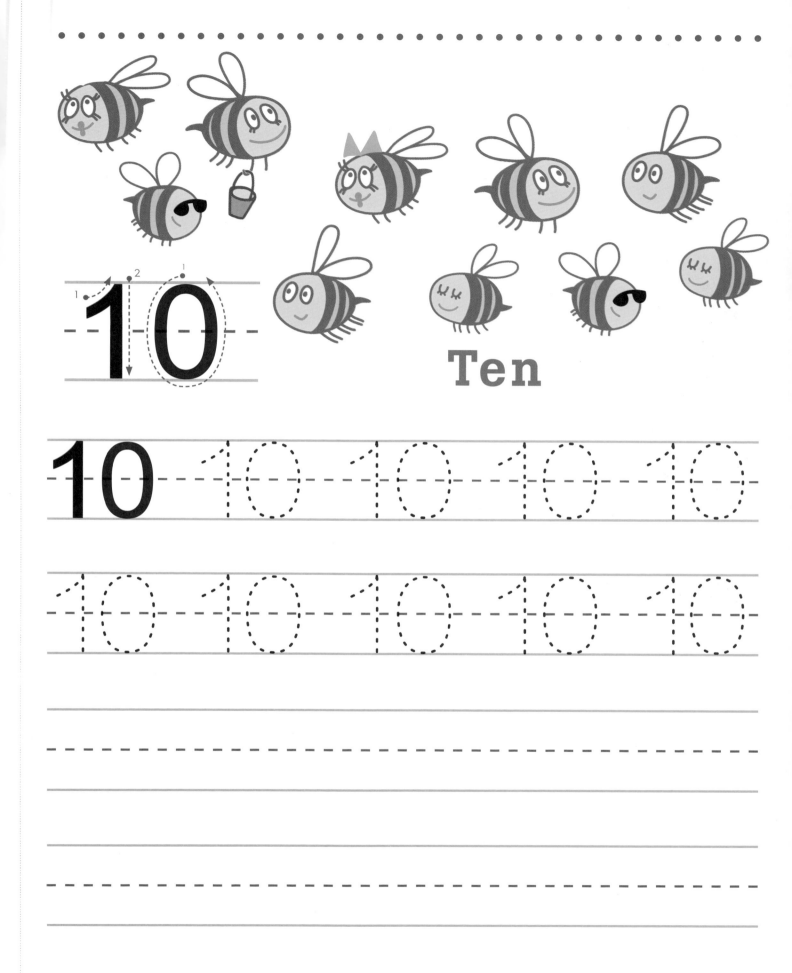

Ten

10 10 10 10 10

10 10 10 10 10

Eleven

Twelve

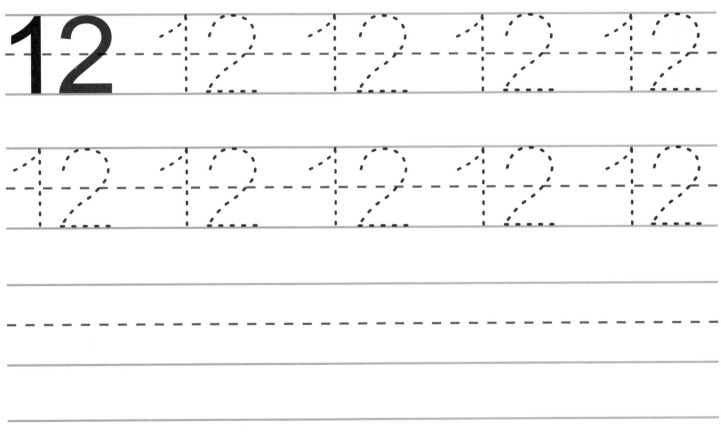

13

Thirteen

13 13 13 13 13

13 13 13 13 13

Fourteen

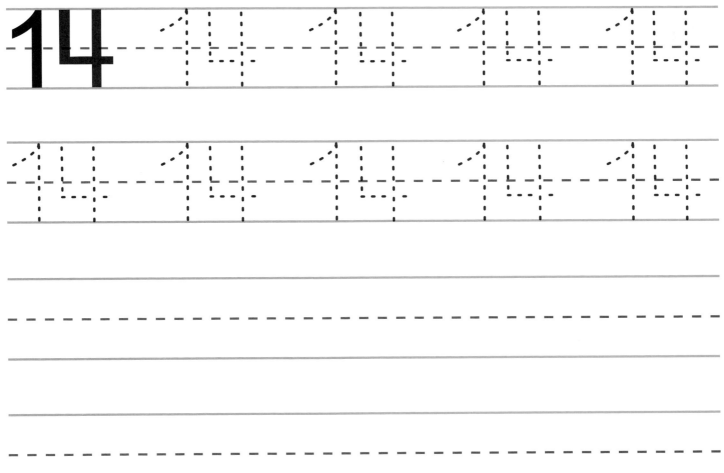

15

Fifteen

Sixteen

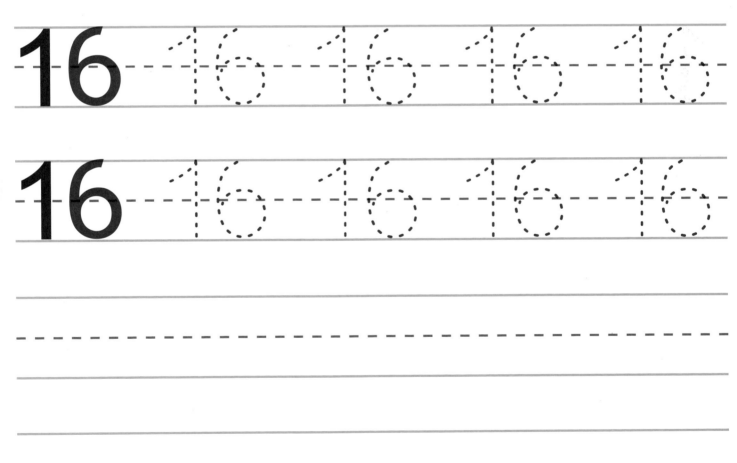

17

Seventeen

17 /7 /7 /7 /7 /7 /7

/7 /7 /7 /7 /7 /7

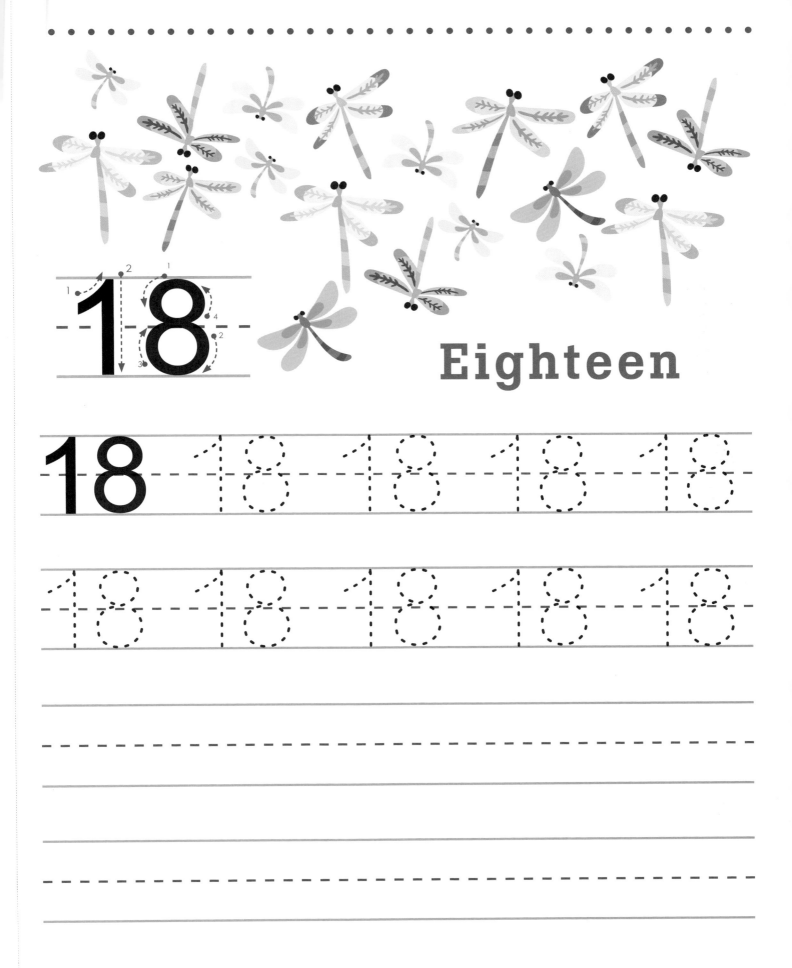

18

Eighteen

18

Nineteen

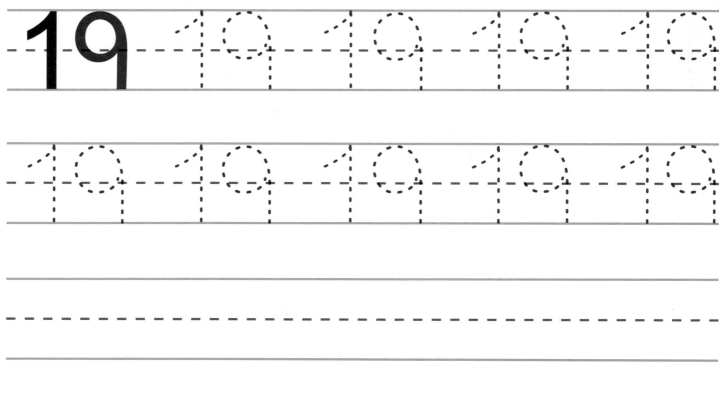

20 Twenty

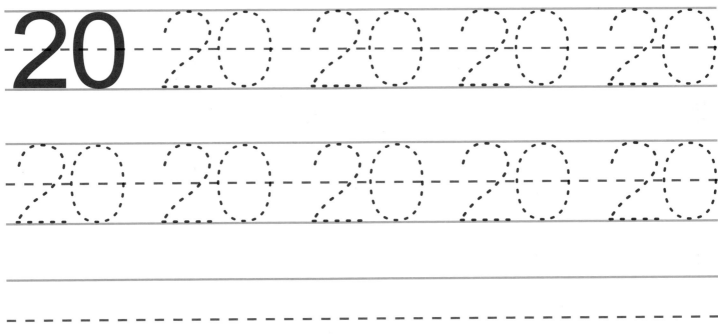

20 20 20 20 20

20 20 20 20 20

Write the Numbers.

1

2

3

4

5

6

7

8

9

10

11 -------------------

16 -------------------

12 -------------------

17 -------------------

13 -------------------

18 -------------------

14 -------------------

19 -------------------

15 -------------------

20 -------------------

Mini-Maze

Help the bird find her nest! Draw a line from 1 to 15 in squares that touch.

	13	12
15	14	11
5	9	10
2	8	6
13	7	3
5	6	2
4	11	14
3	9	
2	1	

Mini-Maze

Help the bunny find his carrots! Draw a line from 1 to 16 in squares that touch.

	14	13	12
16	15	12	11
9	10	11	10
8	1	8	6
7	6	1	3
8	5	3	
9	4	11	
12	3	2	
2	13	1	

How Many Do You See?

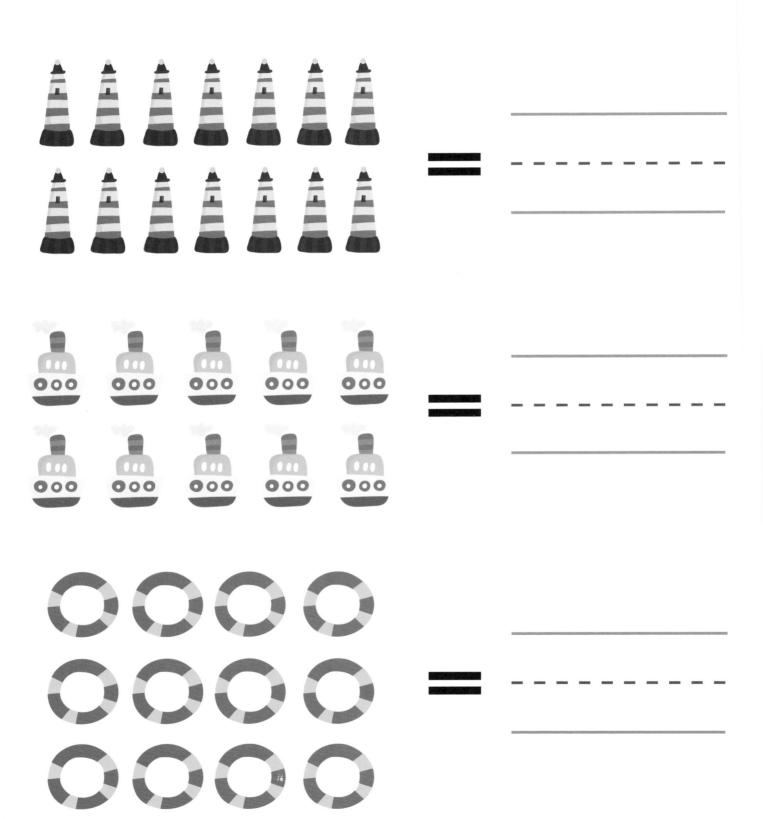

How Many of Each?

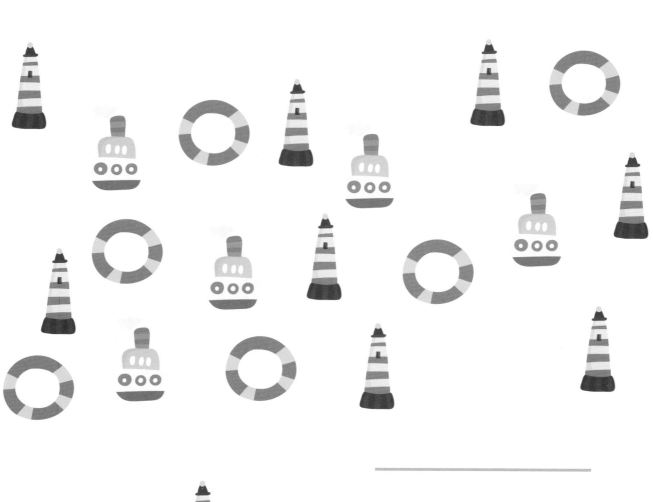

How Many **=** - - - - - - - - - -

How Many **=** - - - - - - - - - -

How Many **=** - - - - - - - - - -

Can You Add These Together?

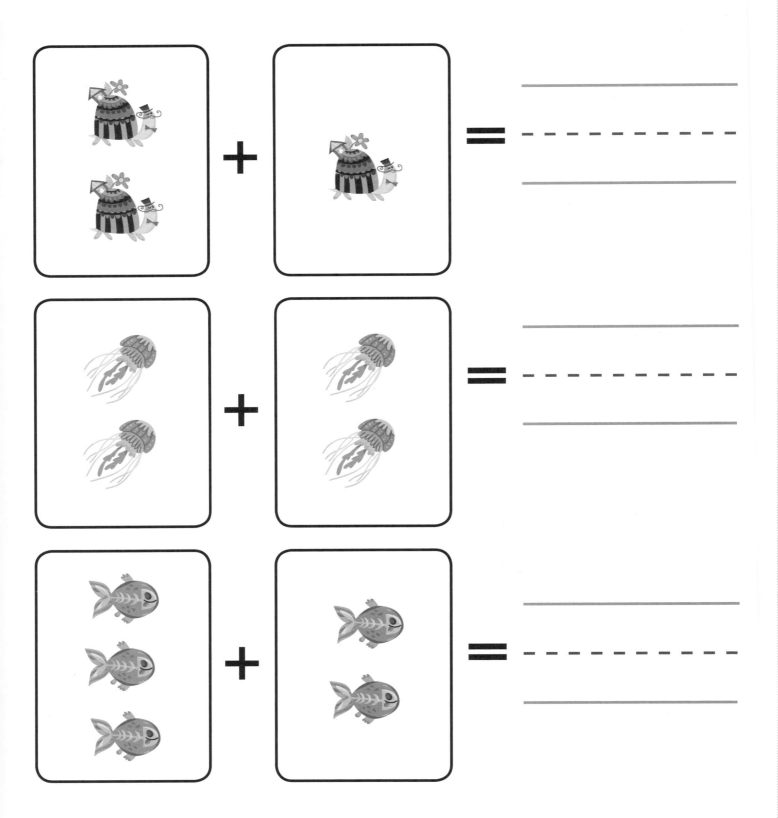

Can You Add These Together?

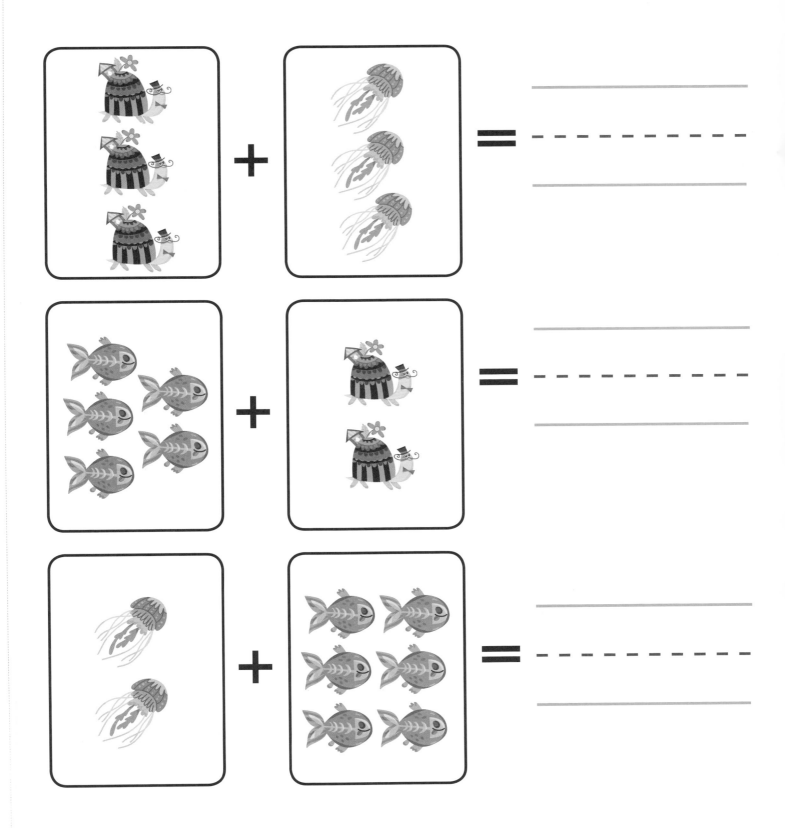

Count the Jellyfish.
Draw a Line to the Correct Number.

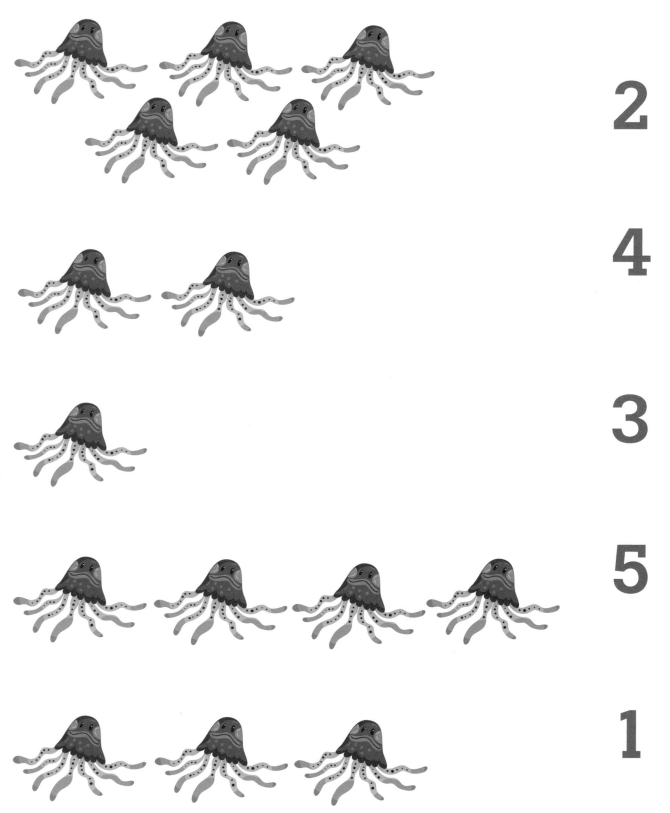

2

4

3

5

1

Count the Gators.
Draw a Line to the Correct Number.

3

5

4

1

2

Count the Pictures.
Circle the Correct Number.

1   2   3

4   5   6

7   8   9

Count the Pictures.
Circle the Correct Number.

1 2 3

4 5 6

7 8 9

How Many Do You See?

How Many Do You See?

Follow the Dots.

Follow the Dots.

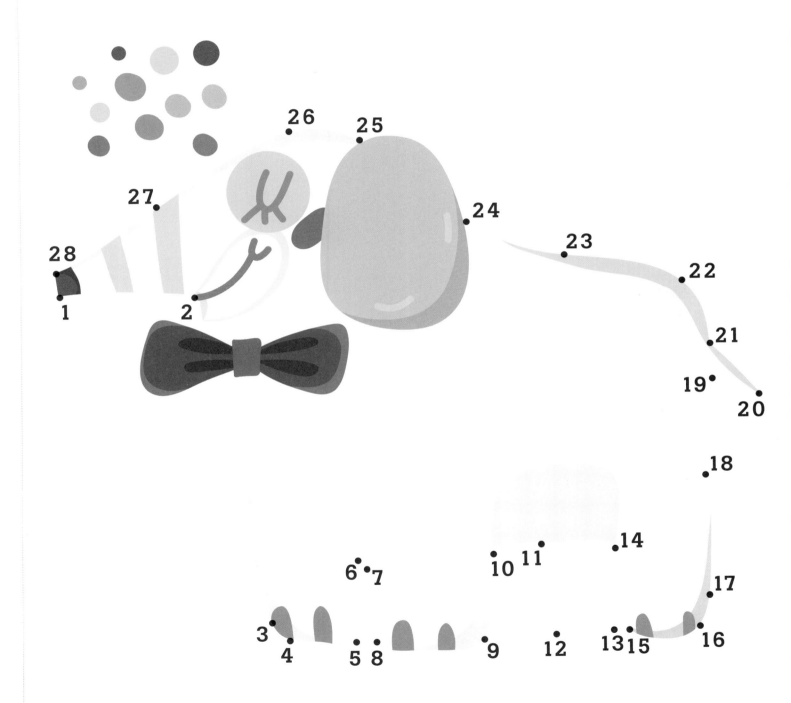

All About Me—in Numbers!

I am _____ years old.

There are _____ people in

my family.

I was born in the year _____.

I have _____ eyes.
(How many?)

_____

- - - - - - - - - - - - - - - - -

I have _____ **toes.**

(How many?)

_____

- - - - - - - - - - - - - - - - -

I have _____ **nose.**

(How many?)

_____

- - - - - - - - - - - - - - - - -

I am _____ **tall.**

Count and Write the
Missing Numbers.

1   _____   3   4   _____

_____   7   8   _____   10

11   _____   13   14   _____

16   _____   _____   19   _____